The Ten Rules of Flute

Techniques for Efficient Instruction Through High school and Beyond

Jason Blank

The Ten Rules of Flute: techniques for efficient instruction through High school and Beyond

Copyright © 2012 by Jason Blank

All rights reserved. No part of this book may be reproduced or transmitted in any form or by any means without written permission from the author.

ISBN (978-1475263152)

Acknowledgements and Dedication

Without my teachers, I wouldn't know which hole to blow in, far less anything else about the flute. So, thank you to Dr. Lynne Cooksey, Ms. Leanne Wistrom, Mr. Jeffrey Khaner, and Ms. Jean Larson Garver for all of your guidance. I realize now that I wasn't the usual student, so I appreciate your patience.

Next, thank you to my family, Heidi, Connor, and Max, who let me sneak away to my office at night to make this book a reality.

Third, great thanks go to all of the directors and parents in Texas who gave me a shot when I was a new teacher. I got my start because of you, purchased my first car, then my first house because of you.

Also, thank you to Qian Ni, owner of Haynes Flutes, who not only gave me a national voice for my teaching, but also taught me a lot about business and people.

However, this book is dedicated to my students. Even though many of you grew both as musicians and people under my direction, I learned more from you than I could ever give in return.

Contents

Introduction 1
Part One: The Ten Rules of Flute 5
The Ten Rules 6
Things to remember while teaching the ten rules 7
Rule #1   10
Rule #2   11
Rule #3   12
Rule #4   14
Rule #5   15
Rule #6   19
Rule #7   22
Rule #8   24
Rule #9   25
Rule #10 27

Part Two: Note Grouping 28
Introduction 29
The General Process 30
For Rhythm 32

Part Three: Scary Topics Made Easy 35
Hand Position 36
Embouchure 39
A Metaphor for Quick Tonguing, double/triple tonguing 43
Singing while Playing and how to teach it 44
Why we call the key "Thumb Bb", not Thumb A# 46
Vibrato 48
Playing in the three registers 54
Words I never use 56
Conclusion, and a Challenge 58

Introduction

Who would benefit from this book?

My principal audience is the educator in a group setting. The educational models in this book install functional behavior patterns in a flute section, quickly and easily, with those behaviors becoming habit just as quickly and easily. However, my hope is that flute teachers and students of all levels will also use the book to invigorate discussion of how we teach and learn.

What this book is not:

Substitute for good private instruction

Instrumental music has been taught for hundreds of years in a private setting for good reason: what we teach is such a complex behavior, and each student is going to have their own needs, strengths and weaknesses. This book is not meant to replace the guidance of a professional in a private lesson environment, nor should be viewed as a "do it yourself" kit for your own playing. Use it this way at your own folly.

However, you'll see that the book mostly focuses on working with a one student at a time, even in the classroom. Almost all of the group concepts are put in after the individual ones, as a wonderful flute section's sound is an emergent property, coming to fruition only when the individual players have the proper skills.

A philosophical text on pedagogy

I trained to play the flute, not teach it. However, I found myself not only teaching private lessons but also masterclasses at public schools, and now universities. Success came upon the realization that I was providing a service. The quality of that educational service, not my ability to play the flute, was my new criteria for success. This became more important upon my appointment as clinician for Haynes Flutes. I would fly into a city and work with a group of flutists for an hour, given only a couple of minutes with each student, aware of the goal: to improve the group in a noticeable and repeatable way.

I needed an engaging way to cause profound changes in my students. The methods in this book were formed "in the trenches", bringing a variety of students to a consistently high level quickly, while keeping it fun. I will leave it to other more qualified people to figure out why my teaching style works, as my job is to help you find an effective teaching structure, then explain the technical aspects behind that structure.

What this book does

- Gives a fundamental framework for beginning flutists through an undergraduate performance degree, using positive commands and humor.
- Restructures much of what you already know about the flute— some of the content might be what you already teach. I have prioritized the fundamentals then supplied a vehicle that is easy to install with students.
- For band directors, the book creates a bridge between what students are learning in their private lessons and your flute section goals.

The dysfunctional feedback loop

Many teachable flute concepts do not work by themselves, but rather must be in balance with what seems to be a non-related concept. If this does not happen, the player will become to reliant on thing being taught. Overdoing something on the flute is often as bad as not doing it at all, so the more the student does what is being taught, the worse they will do.

A great example is the relationship between lips and air. At some point, every student is taught the role the lips serve while playing the flute. Even if breathing and blowing is taught correctly at another juncture, if the air and lips are not taught together, the student will get the impression that the lips are the focus and forget about the air. They will then rely too much on the lips, making it harder to use the correct amount of air, which will then cause increased reliance on the lips again, and so on. I call this phenomena a dysfunctional feedback loop. Even though the content can be correct, if balance is not also taught between that concept and a complimentary one, the result will be a student with tight lips and no air. By teaching concepts in balance with one another, not only will the student be more successful at that moment, but also will have more options, as changing a balance really changes two things at once.

Throughout the book, I will mention these feedback loops-- much of my teaching centers around breaking these cycles.

How this book is structured (and how to use it)

Part one: the ten rules

The ten rules form a basis for generating a strong, flexible tone throughout all octaves of the instrument, then keeping this resonate sound during all types of playing. It was the basis for my national clinic tours with Haynes Flutes and came from my teaching experience in Texas, and now Boston. If you are going to read one section of the book then let it collect dust, read, apply, and live part one. My suggestions for learning part one are as follows:

- Read the ten rules (and laugh, it is encouraged)

- Re-read the ten rules, now with implementation suggestions

- Listen to your students play a section of music, then, using the rules, install some new behaviors. Listen again to the passage. This will prove the effectiveness of the rules to you, giving you a reason to invest in reading the rest of the book.

- Read the analysis, giving a deeper understanding of both the concepts behind the rules, thinking of how the rules can be used together.

- Stack the rules, reinforcing the fundamentals to build an environment of correct execution.

Part two: Note Grouping

In the ten rules, most of the topics either deal directly with air or must be taught in balance with air. In part two, I change another element of playing: time. Although, in the flute player's frame of reference, time moves at a constant rate, the subjective perception of time can change while playing with much benefit.

Part three: scary topics made easy

This section contains responses to the most asked questions after a clinic by educators. Some of the answers are explored applications of the ten rules, others build upon them.

Part One: The Ten Rules of Flute

The ten rules

Rule #1: Always blow your air at a target: band directors make great targets.

Rule #2: Breathe in minty.

Rule #3: Keep the more important thing still—move the less important thing.

Rule #4: The shiny thing should move when you breathe.

Rule #5: Wherever you got rib, you got lung. And you got more in the back than the front.

Rule #6: Consonants are for tonguing, vowels are for playing.

Rule #7: High notes should come out your nose.

Rule #8: Hands and air have nothing to do with each other—flutists are air-pumps with fingers.

Rule #9: Speed while playing is limited by how quickly you can lift your fingers, not by how fast you can put them down.

Rule #10: Soft is the same thing as loud, just quieter: High is the same thing as low, it is just higher.

Things to remember while teaching the "the ten rules"

Your effectiveness is measured by your student's results

I am, as you should be, only concerned with results, defined by how your students play in a concert or at an audition. The only true test of your students is their ability to play under pressure, when their natural state takes over.

Structure is as least as important as content

You probably teach much of the content that is contained in part one of this book. However, the structure containing that content will probably be different. After I had been doing clinics for a while, a sales rep with Haynes or a educational rep from the store that sponsored me would come along to multiple clinics in a city. I felt bad having them hear the same stuff over and over again, so I would change what I said while I taught. Almost always, I would have to reteach the material again. I realized it really wasn't the content that was different, but rather the structure of how the information was transmitted.

Start with the end in mind

Write down the qualities you are looking for in your flute section. Instead of using the rules to "fix problems", use the rules to "nudge" students in the correct direction, building a foundation of correct playing.

Changes must be easy and quickly proven functional to students or the change will be lost

I have seen flute clinics by some very fine musicians where the students sounded better during the clinic. However, soon after the clinician left, the students reverted to their old behavior patterns. Why? I can see a couple of reasons: first, the new behavior was not proven to actually sound better to the student; second, the process to get the desired result seemed harder, or was harder than what they currently do, and finally, the student didn't have an easy to remember trigger to recreate the behavior when the physical feeling was lost.

Assumptions in teaching

My teaching improved exponentially when I embraced the following assumptions:

- Young people think faster than adults, so the window where the student evaluates content is shorter.

- Everyone does what they feel works for them at any moment; otherwise, why would they do it? Any time your student plays, from their point of view, they do what they feel works.

- Good teaching stays far away from value judgement. Instead of "right" and "wrong", there are two subjective models of how to play the flute: one of the teacher, and one of the student. Teaching is coalescing the two models, allowing a flow of functional content from teacher to student, while leaving the musical, creative core of the student intact.

- Playing the flute is easy. When things work right, it looks easy, and should feel easy, so it is useful to think of it as easy.

I suggest thinking deeply about your own assumptions as you start to use the rules.

The rules are meant to be lighthearted and funny.

It is best to move on if a rule isn't working right away. Another rule can always be used, as they are meant to work together, as the rules overlap one another. The teacher is only part of the teaching equation. Just because you think it is the right rule to apply doesn't make it so. It is the right rule if it works. After reading the analysis of each rule, feel free to substitute your own metaphors and images. Nothing is written in stone.

The rules can, and should, be taught from the beginning.

I have a problem leaving out fundamental concepts in the beginning years, only to teach these basics later. This becomes a big problem, as we then have to battle the pre-existing habits above and below that concept. We should not strive to teach "beginning flute", then "getting better flute", followed by "now you deserve good flute". Let us just teach real flute from the beginning, and realize that it is our fault if a beginning class can not grasp the fundamentals of playing the instrument.

Rule #1: Always blow your air at a target: band directors make great targets

Implementation example:

Have the flutist or flute section look at you while blowing while they play. Popular targets are a necktie or between the eyes. You can also raise your hand up, wiggling your fingers to focus students who need an active target.

Analysis

The flute is an air powered device. Contrasting with other woodwind and brasswind instruments, there is almost no resistance in the flute/person system (although, for those who are interested, there is impedance). This means that it takes a lot of air to play the flute: as much as a tuba! However, for most beginning students, their focus is on the physical instrument or the music/method book in front of them. This makes sense, as the instrument and music stand are new to the beginning student and are easily seen, as opposed to internal processes like breathing and body positioning. However, focusing the mind first on something other than air, especially in the first years, cracks the foundation of their playing.

Rule #2: Breathe in minty

Implementation example:

"Have you every been to a fine restaurant, and they gave you a mint at the end of the meal? When you breathe in, can you feel the cold, minty air hit the back of your throat? This is how the air should feel when you breathe in before playing."

Analysis

Before playing, there is the urge to force air into the body, especially when breathing in quickly. The player often accomplishes this by tensing the back of the mouth and throat. Many teachers respond by either telling the student to relax the throat or not to tense. While it is easy to see that "don't tense" is two commands: "tense"+"not", many teachers don't realize that telling a student to relax is processed the same way. Music, like the rest of reality, is comprised of opposites, the most important being something and nothing. By telling the student to relax, you are using a something to describe a process dealing in the opposite-- nothing. Telling a nervous student to do nothing is almost impossible. It is more functional to substitute a process they student can hang on to.

For the air to feel "minty", the throat must be open, the tongue low, and the air must be traveling quickly, which are all key elements taught in breathing texts. This circumvents telling them to "not do something" to do with breathing; rather, it sets up the correct structure, rediscovering something they once knew how to do: to breathe like a baby.

Rule #3: Keep the more important thing still—move the less important thing

Implementation example

When putting the flute to the lips, watch for head movement. If the student moves the head while bringing up the flute, ask "which is more important, the flute or you? You are more important. Always bring the less important thing to the more important". Usually, the student will still not realize their head moves, so a mirror or the feedback of other students can be used.

Analysis

This rule presupposes you know what is more or less important. As I stated in the introduction, educators will introduce a "fix" to a problem only to inject unforeseen consequences, leading to more fixes, creating a feedback loop that causes anxiety in the student. This usually ends with poor air and tight lips that feed on each other, manifesting as out of tune, quiet playing with no speed or color.

In talking with directors across the country, the following emerged as desired qualities for a flute section:

- Appropriate flute tone, given the musical texture called for in the music
- Intonation
- Even, fluid technique

All of these depend on a quality, constant supply of air, as well as relaxed, toned fingers. Incorrect body structure tightens the hands, as well as makes inhaling and exhaling more difficult. The flute supplies none of the air it uses; rather, all air flow is generated from the player. When playing any wind instrument, there is an optimal body structure, which maintains optimal air flow, releases the tongue, and keeps the fingers loose and ready to play. This is the most basic building block on which everything else is built, and nothing introduced afterwards should interfere with this structure, including the flute.

I will not go into a detailed exploration of posture while playing the flute. There are very good texts on this subject, as well as people who have devoted their entire careers studying posture, both with and without an instrument. My purpose here is to illustrate the importance of prioritizing goals in education, and being aware of these priorities while adding new concepts.

This rule originally was "bring the shiny thing to you", as it illustrated a very easy to teach concept, while prioritizing the student over the instrument. You might still catch me saying this in a clinic, as it works very well. However, I realized there is a more general concept at work.

The most effective teachers prioritize instrumental fundamentals, then again with the musical needs of the ensemble. Always teach to reinforce basics while adding new concepts so they do not interfere with concepts below them. You will then have a flute section that performs how they practice, reliably and effectively.

Also, under pressure, the basics remain. When the chaotic storm of public performance arrives, a strong foundation will at the least make a shelter in which to return, and, at its best, will reinforce the entire structure, so you may sculpt air with your group while the hurricane swirls around you.

Rule #4: The shiny thing should move when you breathe

Implementation example:

"Can you open your mouth? Good job. What moved? The jaw moved—you only have one jaw. Where does the air go in when you are playing the flute? The mouth. Can you relax your jaw, causing it to open? Good. This is an efficient (quick) way to open your mouth. What is attached to your jaw when you play? The shiny thing. So the shiny thing should move as you inhale.

Analysis

Efficiency works to your advantage, as this rule as an extension of rule #3—move the less important object as opposed to the more important.

Keeping the flute still while raising the head engages the muscles of the neck and upper back. This tension restricts air, which by now you know I think is bad. The lungs will not be able to expand freely. Dropping the jaw is how we breathe without the flute, so why should it change when we introduce something less important than us?

Also, dropping the jaw clears tension out of the mouth that builds while playing a long time or after a series of quick breaths. The drop should be large to start so the concept is clear, but will become smaller with practice. The important thing is that the movement always comes from the jaw. It might seem slower in the beginning with large movements but will eventually be quicker, as the opening of the mouth will accelerate from gravity.

Rule #5: Wherever you got rib, you got lung. And you got more in the back than the front.

Implementation example:

Have the student play a simple passage, noticing the quality of sound. Then, have the student feel their ribs in the front, explaining that there is more lung in the back. The student should then repeat the passage, concentrating on breathing into the back. Without holding the breath, the student should just reverse the direction of the air. This should be done several times, each time the student noticing a richer sound, as well as a feeling of more air to use while playing.

Analysis

Humans are very visual, so we place a lot of importance on things in front of us. The trade off is that we forget what is behind us, both inside and outside of our bodies. The ribs surround the lungs, giving us a good guide as to where the lungs reside. Looking at an anatomy chart or feeling your own ribs, notice that the ribcage resides both higher and lower in the torso than students think, and the ribs flair more in the back than in the front. If students don't know where the ribs are, they will probably restrict the natural expansion that should happen when they inhale.

Think of the lungs as a balloon. It is harder to blow up the balloon with our hands around it. Our ribs and the muscles around them become the hands around the balloon, restricting the inflation of the lungs. A full breath will not be possible, limiting their air supply. Compounding this, the person will feel full of air prematurely, so they redefine a full breath to be smaller than what is possible, forming a dysfunctional feedback loop between ribs and lung capacity. The lungs, with associated fascia, are just like the skin of a balloon, and will stretch while inflated.

The natural elasticity helps push the air out of the body, much like a balloon deflating out the end.

Many times a student will breathe in, only to have the shoulders rise while inhaling. Most teachers have a knee jerk reaction to this, telling the student not to raise the shoulders, a form of negative reinforcement. The student will then force the shoulders down, further limiting their air supply.

A better solution lies in an understanding of tension in the body. The ribs hang from the spine, so movement of the spine is related to the inflation of the lungs. Also, there is no weight bearing skeletal connection between the shoulders and the spine-- the collar bone doesn't count, as it is just a "door stop", limiting the back and forth motion of the shoulder.

The shoulders only move when we breathe because we lock the muscles in the upper back, connecting things that are unrelated. So, if the shoulders move, it is because we are connecting the shoulders with muscle attached to the skeletal structure holding the breathing apparatus in place. Feeling the air enter the body through the mouth, then expanding from the middle of the back outward should disconnect the mental image linking the shoulder to back, and the student will then be able to take a full breath without the shoulders moving.

Another principle is at work: the spine shortens during inhalation, and lengthens during exhalation; that is, you get shorter when you breathe in and taller when you exhale. A helpful model is as follows: Imagine the body as a water filled sphere, at rest on the ground. If a force f is applied downward on the sphere, assuming the ground is solid so there is a counteracting normal force, the ball will deform perpendicular to the line of our force, which we will name f_2.

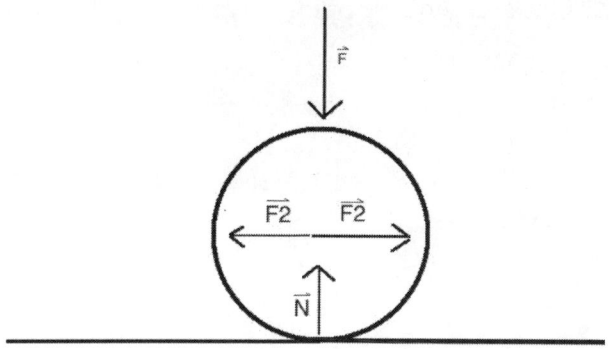

This same force f2 occurs in our body, except it is caused by the air coming in our body. The ribs flair, and the spine compresses from the tension.

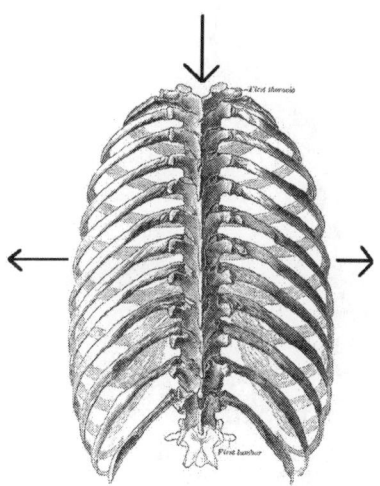

However, ask most students and teachers. They will tell you the opposite occurs. The problem is, if you believe the body works in a certain way, your mind will attempt to make that model become reality. Let us look at what happens if the spine expands while breathing in:

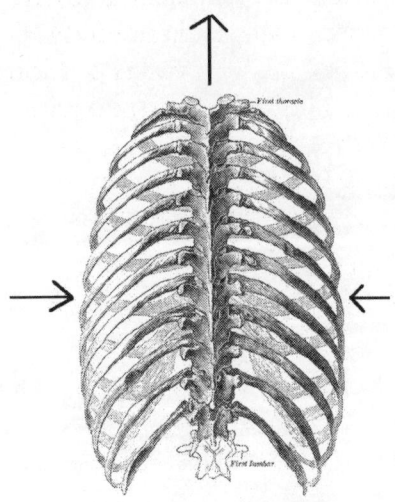

The spine will cause tension on the ribs, preventing them from flaring properly, which creates tension, reducing the maximum air volume from the player.

For teaching young students, I recommend "hulking out". If you don't know what this is, a simple web search for The Incredible Hulk will help. The concept is simple- nice guy, turns green, back rips clothing. If you think of ripping your shirt or jacket by curling the shoulders forward and in while flaring the back, you will feel both the disconnect between the shoulder girdle and spine, as well as the tension you would cause in the back by not letting the ribs flair. Relax, coming back to a point of good posture, then breathe in, letting the air mimic the feeling you had in your back while hulking. If you don't hold your breath before playing, air will rip across the flute.

Rule #6: Consonants are for tonguing, vowels are for playing

This is a really a two part rule, but these actions are commonly taught as one, especially in a group setting. Many teachers teach tonguing with a "ta" or "tee" syllable, when all that is needed is the American pronunciation of the letter "T". The vowel portion assists in tone production and response, and has little to do with articulation. I include them in one rule as they are often discussed together; however, I will separate them in implementation and analysis, as it is useful to change each independently.

Vowel opening

Implementation example

Say "ooo". Now say "eee". Now, say "ooo" then "eee" without moving your lips. What moved? The tongue. Now, remember that low register notes are "ooo" notes, and middle register notes are "eee" notes.

Analysis

When playing, the air column inside of the flute vibrates. The air inside the player also vibrates, and any change in the volume or shape of the air column inside the body will effect the tone quality and response of the player/flute system. The easiest way to institute these changes are by adjusting the mouth and throat.

At any point in time, the inside of the mouth is held in a position that, if you are talking, would approximate a spoken vowel. Teaching vowel openings is very functional, as they describe internal changes that neither you nor your students can see.

For the low register, an "ooo" or sometime "ah" syllable works very well. The goal is the lower the back of the tongue, allowing the mouth and throat to be as open as possible for maximum airflow across the flute. With this structure in place, the student, with relaxed lips, will be able to play loud in the low register.

In the middle register, an "eeeeeeeee" is used. The student should feel the vowel sound very forward in the mouth, as if the tone bounces off the back of the teeth. In general, the middle of the tongue will be high, yet the front and back of the tongue will be low. You might be trying to replicate this as you read the previous sentence. See how much easier it is just to use the vowel opening than discussing the position of the tongue? The high register is covered in rule #7.

Tonguing

Implementation example – This is to be used either when the student can not tongue quickly or the notes do not respond when the tempo increases.

Have the student play the passage without the tonguing at all, putting space between the notes. They should "Puff" into the flute. If the notes do not start, change the vowel opening. If the notes have tails of sound on the end, connecting one note to the next, especially at high speed, remind the student that to separate notes, just stop blowing. The tonguing can be added afterwards, when it sounds correct with puffing.

Analysis

One of the themes in this book is that air makes the flute go. From this, you should eliminate anything that impedes the flow of air in the flute/player system. This includes the tongue— although tonguing happens many times at the beginning of playing, it is a bad idea to use articulation to make the flute respond. Air flow causes sound, not the tongue.

Instead, it is much better to have the air flow correctly using proper body positioning. In the implementation example, the student divorces tonguing from the process of making the instrument speak. If the student has response issues, particularly in the low register, the vowel opening should be adjusted, so that the flute speaks easily. The tonguing can then be added, completing the sound. This is what teachers used to refer to as "tonguing on top of the air".

If the student has trouble separating the notes while puffing, it is an example of making something simple very complex. How do you stop playing the flute? You stop blowing. It really is that simple. Often times the limit to how quickly a student can play fast staccato passages is not their tongue, but rather how quickly they can stop the air in between notes.

There is an added benefit to this approach for advanced students. Different consonants can be used to articulate the flute, especially useful in baroque music. The reliance on the tongue to start the sound limits the player to only the harder consonants, violating a fundamental principal: physical limitations of the flute/player system should effect the interpretation of music as little as possible.

Rule #7: High notes should come out your nose

Implementation example:

"Have you ever been drinking soda then laughed, making the soda come out your nose? Can you feel the bubbles of the soda now? Thinking of that feeling, play (insert something with high register playing) again, making the notes come out your nose."

Analysis

As when we sing, the body resonates when playing the flute. Depending on the register, the student should focus on different parts of the body. From rule 6, we learned that the the vowel opening, which is controlled by the shape of the mouth, tongue and throat, facilitate the low and middle register. We can expand this, focusing of the chest cavity when playing low and the mouth when in the middle register.

The 3rd octave responds best when the sinuses sympathetically vibrate. Think of the sinuses as an "echo" chamber, allowing more air to resonate inside the body. This will occur when the soft pallet, located in the back roof of the mouth, rises. However, most students don't have the sensory awareness to do this, so I ask them to metaphorically aspirate the notes through the nose, causing the same physical state.

Every student can implement rule #7, but teaching it causes the most perplexed looks from both students and teachers, making this is a good time to discuss reasons for resistance to any of the rules. There are two types of resistance that manifest the same way: "this isn't going to work". In one, students limit themselves because they don't believe that change is as easy as imagining something while they play. In the other, students feel pressure, either outward or inward, to never make a mistake or sound bad, even it is first step down a path toward better, more reliable playing. This pressure closes the mind and makes the student retreat further into their own model of playing, instead of going toward the teacher's model.

No matter the reason, there are two sentence patterns I use either together or separately to eliminate barriers between what students think they can do and the possible. First, ask them if they think they can do it. When they answer "no", tell them "believe that you can do it, then do it anyway". The incongruence of this statement usually opens their mind. The second pattern is "imagine it is me controlling the flute, not you. Play this again, thinking the rule, and if it doesn't work, blame me, not you". Giving students someone to blame grants them permission to fail, lifting a limitation for success.

Rule #8: Hands and air have nothing to do with each other—flutists are air-pumps with fingers

Implementation example:

Use with students who can play a held note with a great sound but whose sound suffers when playing technical passages. Have them play the first note of the problem passage and hold it out with a great sound, then again while imagining they are moving their fingers, comparing the quality of sound. Repeat until the tone quality is the same, tell them rule #8, then have students play the passage as written, this time with the same air they used on the single note.

Analysis

Students and teachers often connect things that have nothing to do with the other. Someone can play a note on the flute with a great sound, and when I stand next to them and depress another key, the tone quality doesn't change. Why then should it change when the same person blows and moves their fingers? This can be cathartic for many students, and I suggest playing this "duet" with the student, or have students partner up and have one student blow while the other pushes down the keys.

Often times the fear of playing an incorrect note causes cautious air. Ironically, this type of blowing usually compounds the problem, introducing a dysfunctional feedback loop of cautious air causing more problems, which then causes more cautious air. The answer to many technical demands on the flute is more air, then getting out of the way of that air. The following metaphor can help drive the point home: There is only one note in music. We just adjust the pitch of that note with our fingers, matching what is on the page.

Rule #9: Speed while playing is limited by how quickly you can lift your fingers, not put them down

Implementation Example:

When a student is having trouble playing a passage quickly or if they seem like they are working hard while playing a passage at speed, ask them to focus on the fingers which lift the keys to change notes while feeling the keys underneath their fingers.

Analysis

The muscles that close the hand are much stronger than those which open it. This makes sense, as in times of duress, it is much more important to be able to grab something quickly and hold on than to let something go. This holds true on the flute, as even with the added force the springs attached to the keys provide, we can put keys down more quickly than we can lift them.

Focusing on lifting the fingers will also improve the student's touch on the instrument. When flutists play fast passages, there is a tendency to tense the shoulders and arms. Locking the upper body further limits the speed the hands can be released. Concentrating on the lifting of the fingers relaxes the hands, arms, along with the rest of the upper body, leaving the student ready to move air and wiggle fingers efficiently.

This is also a good way to teach how far the fingers should come up while playing. Any movement of the finger beyond the stopping point of the key is wasted twice, as the finger continues to travel up, then must travel again through this space to start the key on its way back down to seat. So it is best to keep the fingers very close to the keys while playing. If the student focuses on lifting the fingers while still feeling the keys, they will develop the correct feel for the instrument. In this way, technique will look easy to the audience while relaxing the student under what would otherwise be stressful playing.

Rule #10: Soft is the same thing as loud, just quieter: High is the same thing as low, it is just higher

Implementation Example:

If a student can transition well from the middle to high register at a loud dynamic but not a soft one, tell the student to play the passage loud first, then imagine the passage is loud while playing it soft. This might take a couple attempts, but once the student truly believes they are loud when they play soft, the playing will become effortless.

Analysis

Labels can be a very powerful thing, both to ourselves and our students. Many students have built in habits associated with playing soft or high that interfere with proper playing. However, these habits are not as strong with loud playing in the middle register. Most students learn at least one way to play both soft and high, as well as low and soft, but they tend to overdo the physical behaviors for the intended goal when dealing with these extremes of the instrument or when under pressure.

Playing the flute is a very complex motion, enough so that the mind can't focus on each of the seemingly infinite things needed to play the instrument. So we learn a couple of the actions, then group them together. These groups are eventually joined into the one action of playing the instrument. When there is a flaw in one of these groups, it is often more useful to apply a different group that works instead of tearing apart the offending group.

Part Two: Note Grouping

Note grouping

Introduction

Imagine you or one of your students was going to learn the following musical example from the C major Bach flute sonata:

How would you do this? Many of you, after scanning it for basic information, would turn on the metronome and start slugging away, slowly at first, then moving the tempo faster. But what if you only had five minutes to learn it? I teach a system, which will allow you to learn music quickly, minimize note errors, even out technical passages, and improve rhythmic precision and memorization, while giving you clues into how to phrase the passage. Sounds too good to be true? Keep reading.

Let's look at the example again. It is all sixteenth notes, but why are they beamed into groups of four? The beams show one possible position of the beats in the measure, so we see instantly where the clicks or beeps of the metronome could fall. However, there are implications to organizing the musical data in this way: first, notes on the beat look more important than the ones they surround; next, the space between each beamed set artificially separates each set of notes; lastly, having a first note of a beat be the first note of a beamed set suggests it is the beginning of something. The problem with these implications is that every one of them is false.

Allow me to rewrite the passage in the following way:

Even though this looks different, it should sound identical to someone listening while feeling easier to play evenly. However, this presentation will cause problems with both teaching a student rhythm, as well rehearsing in a group. There should be a way that allows us to retain the visual organization of beats while counteracting the unforeseen implications of how we print musical data on the page. This way is called note grouping.

The General Process

It might be easiest to show the general process first, then apply it to the Bach passage. With any section of music, use the following algorithm to define and practice the groups:

1. Define a beat, as it applies to your analysis.
2. Starting with the 2nd note/rest within the 1st beat to be grouped, draw a bracket either on the page or in your mind, inclusive of that note/rest, through the 1st note/rest of the next beat.
3. If your termination note/rest is greater or equal to the length of your defined beat, either continue the bracket through 1st note/rest of the next beat or refine the value of your beat. Let us define this bracketed section as a note group.
4. Play each note group, stopping between them, taking as much time needed between note groups to ensure that each group's rhythm is correct in relation to the others notes in the group. More difficult groups may be practiced individually until all groups feel easy. I can't stress enough that you can take as much time as you want in between the groups.
5. Turn on the metronome at a tempo slow enough to allow you to play the notes with no breaks between groups but still able to think of the notes in their newly defined relationships.
6. You will now be able to work up the passage quickly and easily, only limited in speed by how fast you can continue to associate the material into note groups.

Applying this process to our example, the groups are as follows:

Have one of your flutists learn the above passage using the note grouping process. They will find it "strangely easy" to play even and fluid, especially at tempi faster than would have been uncomfortable in the past.

Why I teach stopping in between the groups.

Note grouping came from the Philadelphia pedagogical tradition at the Curtis Institute of Music, where it is still taught to flutists and wind quintets. Brackets are drawn to help the student conceptualize the groups. Often, this is taught as a duet, with the student and teacher alternating between groups.

I changed this process by having the student stop playing in between groups. When I began to teach, students would have trouble thinking the note groups while playing the continuous line of music. Even if the groups were conceptualized, students really didn't believe the notes in the groups were really connected. Breaking after each group forces the student to associate the correct notes together.

Pausing also gives the student plenty of time to look at the upcoming group, minimizing learning errors while retaining the rhythm within each group. This process is improved if the pauses are thought of as outside of the passage of time while playing. It is like hitting the pause button on a DVD player: time stops in the flow of the movie, and the time counter, along with the actors on the screen, freezes. So, with the flute, the time of the music only flows when the student is playing a group.

The most important benefit of using this start/stop method is that it drives home a powerful assumption in music -- the beat is always the end of something, never the beginning. Mr. John Krell, formally with The Philadelphia Orchestra, had a wonderful analogy that I alter slightly and use quite often: imagine crossing a river for the first time by jumping from stone to stone. You jump then land on each passing rock. Where your foot falls is the beat in music, the end of jump/land process. I extend this concept-- if you had to pause to see where there next foot will fall, where you do pause: after your foot has landed, or in midair? You can stay on each rock as long as you wish as it doesn't alter the physics of the jump itself.

Using note grouping for correct rhythm

The note grouping technology also can decipher tricky rhythms. Notice how the mind reorganizes the following rhythmic data using the provided groups:

Notice that the last example has two layers of groups, dependent on the definition of the beat. This can aid in learning particularly tricky rhythms without sounding "metonomic" in performance.

Breathing implications in note grouping

Teaching where to breathe while playing can be very frustrating. Often, the student is left to extrapolate general principals from breath marks their teacher has written onto the music. We can divide breathing opportunities into two categories. The first are places where the breathing is implied by phrasing-- students should drink deeply from the air where there is a comma or period in the musical sentence. The other is when there isn't enough air to comfortably survive to the next punctuation mark in the music. Here we sip at the air, only taking in enough to get us where we need to go. It is usually these points that confuse students; however, the answer becomes clear with groupings. You may breathe anywhere you wish, as long as it is done in between groups.

Grouping for Memorization

Memorizing music is the bane of most music students' existence. Even though it is a skill, students shy away from something that can be improved as easily as tone or technique. This is because most students, to memorize music, use either a kinesthetic method, commonly called finger memory, or a visual one, called "I can picture the printed music in my head". Both of these methods, because the music data is divided into beats, causes memory to be a two part process: the student must first translate the written page into something flowing through time in their mind, then must memorize that translation. Note grouping offers a way to bypass the translation of the written page.

In the beginning, when memorization is a chore to be done after music has been otherwise learned, I suggest memorizing a section of music at a time broken into groups, then, without the score, working on reducing the time in between groups until there is a smooth line. More advanced students, who should be working on memory while they learn the music, can work on the memory from the initial sectioning of music into groups.

Note grouping also checks how well music has been memorized. Take any music you think you have from memory, then play a passage, starting and stopping in between the groups. This will very quickly show you the holes in your memorization.

Integrating note grouping into the classroom

Once the general concept has been discussed at the whiteboard, blackboard, or chalkboard, note grouping can be very fun to teach to a group of students. Some ways I have used in clinics or group lessons include:

- Students in chair order take a turn playing a group.

- Half an instrument section plays a group, then the other half plays the next.

- In passages where two instrument sections double a line, have the one play the first group, then the other play the next, back and forth through the passage. Starting out, there can be a break between the groups, working toward dovetailing the groups together.

- With scales or other technical exercises, choose random members of the ensemble to play each group in order. This can be predetermined, or on the fly. Don't forget the percussion: they should play the rhythm on their pads or instruments.

Automatically feeling the note grouping takes some time, but this section should get you and your students off to a good start. Obviously the more you bring it up, the easier it will become with your students, so keeping it fun is important. The number of ways it can be used with your group is only limited by your imagination. It is worth it.

Part Three: Scary Topics Made Easy

Scary topics made easy

As I stated in the introduction, this section is a collection of frequently asked questions from my clinics. The answers to many of the questions are either applications or derivations of the ten rules. Others, honestly, are subjects that I thought should be in the book.

Hand position

There are a couple of different approaches as to how to place the hands on the flute. I usually teach one based on relaxation and natural body positioning.

Positioning the right hand

- Shake out the right hand, letting it go limp by your side.

- Tuck the thumb inward, keeping the rest of the hanging arm relaxed.

- Move the right hand onto the flute, placing the fingers as to cover the holes on an open hole instrument.

- Untuck the thumb, letting it rest on the flute in the most comfortable position without altering the structure you just built with the rest of the hand.

If there one step is done incorrectly, the student should start over at the beginning. This takes discipline, but the steps are made to build upon one other.

Everyone's hands and arms are different, so the priority here is to place the fingers in a way that is natural, then letting the thumb support that structure. Forget the pictures shown in most beginning method books-- using the above method will yield a hand position where the fingers have a natural curve and the hand is relaxed, while balancing the flute.

Eating the flute vs nibbling with the right hand

Many students, especially beginners, will let the flute rest too far along the thumb. Worrying about supporting the flute, they place the thumb first, then either curl the fingers back into position on the flute or let the fingers splay onto the instrument, forming a hand position more appropriate to the bagpipe. I call either of these positions "eating the flute with the hand", and both cause dysfunctional tension schemes in the body. Also, by resting the flute too close to the joint in the middle of the thumb, the flute has a tendency to roll over the joint into the depression after it. This is like having the flute at the top of a small hill, having to always fight to keep the flute from rolling down. In our case, the fingers fight the rolling of the flute, leading to slow, tense, difficult sounding technique, as well as an imbalance in the body.

When you come across a student eating the flute with the right hand, explain to them that the hand should be dining at a fine restaurant, where it is impolite to put too much food in your mouth at a time. Rather, they should nibble at the instrument with the finger pads and pad of the thumb, not allowing the flute to come into the "mouth" made by the hand. Then, take them through the process above for placing the right hand on the instrument, using the "nibble check" for feedback.

Positioning the Left Hand

- Shake out the left hand, letting it go limp by your side.

- Imagine a rod going through your forearm into the hand, so the wrist can't move.

- Holding the flute up to the lips with the right hand, use an arcing motion to bring the left hand onto the flute. The space between the first and second knuckle of the index finger, counting from the palm, should touch first, then the fingers should touch, covering the holes (or imaginary ones if it is a closed hole flute). Finally imagine there is a weight on a string hanging down from the elbow. Allow the weight to drop the elbow straight down by relaxing the shoulder. This will allow the thumb to find a comfortable position on either of the keys it operates.

Straight wrist vs bent wrist

Nearly all student flutes, and now a majority of professional ones, come with an offset G key, which allow the wrists to be straight while playing. You can feel the reason for this with a simple exercise: with your wrist straight, wiggle your fingers. Now bend your wrist and do the same thing. Which feels better?

However, there is a technique for playing the inline G flute, which involves a bent left wrist along with a special shape to the thumb. I have no problem with this, but it is taught incorrectly so often, especially in the group setting, that I consider it beyond the scope of this book. Unless you are in a pocket of the country where you have access to a professional with knowledge of this specific hand position, I suggest you plug the G key of all inline flutes in your band, then teach the straight wrist position.

The position of the flute in relation to the lip and the floor

Many people are quite adamant that, if the head is straight, the flute must be perpendicular to the floor. I do not agree, as there are many factors which determine this angle, such as lip shape, formation of hole in the lips left to right, and the player's body conformation. I do think there is a second angle that gets shortchanged yet is much more important, shown in the diagram on the next page:

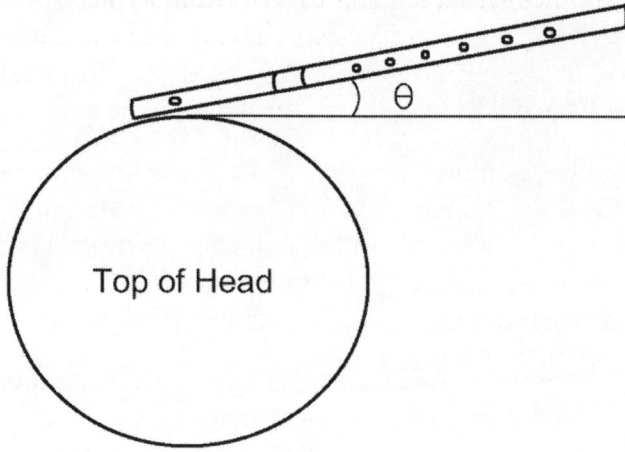

I have heard too many educators force students to keep the flute "straight" while the student has the instrument almost pressed up against their body. Just as clarinetists or oboists do not play with their instruments up against their body, neither should the flutist.

There is no angle theta which is ideal, as it will be different based on the lips and arm length. However I suggest the following as a minimum: when looking forward while playing, you should see the right hand on the flute out of the corner of the eye. If this is not the case, angle the flute on the lips by having the student push gently forward with their right hand.

Embouchure: the one word that messes up more flute students and confuses teachers and conductors than any other

Why I never use the word

I've found using the word embouchure causes tension in the face. Even though it is used with the best of intentions, every time I say "embouchure", everyone subconsciously contorts their face. The tension does not allow flutists to use the proper volume of air, and the tone becomes weak, leading to a dysfunctional feedback loop of more tension and less air. The end result is a player who relies on lips instead of air to play the flute. Priorities become out of whack, leading to a sharp, shrill high register, partnered with a flat, soft low register.

A specific definition

If forced to define embouchure, I would say the following: "Embouchure is the dynamic relationship between the lips and the air that passes through them, achieving a specific purpose in the flute/player system". So, if lemon juice is the tension in the lips, air is the sugar that turns the whole thing into aural lemonade.

Isn't that a mouthful? Even though I wrote the last paragraph, I would have trouble using it in a way to the flute. I suggest substituting the following metaphors for embouchure, which all cause positive changes in the student.

Useful metaphors in place of Embouchure

The Moo Mouth
Have the student hold their mouth natural and relaxed, with the lips lightly touching. While they say "moo", they should feel the mouth part slightly when the air escapes. They should also feel vibration around the center of the lips. Wherever the vibration occurs should be where the lips shape the air leaving the mouth.

Kissing the note
At the basic level, this is best taught as a method for tapering a note. Have the student start by playing a high register note in a full forte. Then, the student should reduce the air as the lips come forward, with the corners of the mouth coming together, as if you are attempting to kiss the flute. The goal is to have the air reducing to zero while the lips keep the note from disappearing. It might take a couple of practice sessions to balance the air with the lips.

The lips can be set in the forward position for starting soft on a note or can be used for register changes at a given air level. Remember that the air must always be balanced for the given position of the lips. Be aware that this forward position should not become the default position for the lips, as the air will reduce, forming a dysfunctional feedback loop.

The lip movement should be large and visible when the exercise is performed correctly. It is diagnostic when a student has trouble moving the lips forward, as this is usually a sign of too much tension in the corners of the mouth. Working on kissing notes away will develop a supple and flexible lip shape for playing the flute.

Smiling and how to work with and around it

We want our flutists to be happy; however, most flutists agree that the the corners of the lips, as a base position, should not be pulled back and upward. Rather, the standard position of the lips should be mostly relaxed, with only enough tension to shape the hole as the air passes through them. That being said, you will be teaching flutists who smile when they play. The solution I see most often involves telling the student the "right" way to hold the lips, then lots of reminding to relax the lips. This often turns into a lot of reminding and usually doesn't work, as student will often hear fuzzy playing as they relearn how to hold the lips and will then go back to smiling, especially when they are nervous.

Instead, I suggest discussing the moo mouth, doing lots of kissing while playing, and, most importantly, using the ten rules to get the student blowing more air into the flute. Many students who smile while playing are caught in a feedback loop of air and lips. Having them just blow more will give instant feedback as to whether the lips are relaxed or not.

Side blowing and other witch hunts

I once attended a school rental meeting where kids were tested for which instruments fit them the best. I was appalled when one student's dreams of playing the flute were shattered when someone told them that they should pick a different instrument because of their lip shape. The student had a "tear drop" in the middle of their top lip. I asked to work with the student for a couple of minutes, and, in that time, they could make a wonderful, strong sound. All that was needed for success was minty breathing, some moo mouth, and blowing at a target, which happened to be my tie.

Remember that the person is more important than the flute. If the hole naturally occurs to the left or right when doing the moo mouth, then this is perfectly correct for that student. The angle of the flute to the lip, the level of kissing the flute, and the vowel opening will just change to accommodate.

A Metaphor for Quick tonguing, double/triple tonguing

I am commonly asked how to improve the speed and quality of double and triple tonguing. Many students and teachers feel that focusing on the tongue will solve the problem. It won't. In general, the more you focus on the tongue, the more the top speed will lower. The key is to focus on air.

Air makes the flute go. Everything regarding playing or teaching the flute starts with air. Therefore, if you think of the tongue as an air powered device, the tongue will not get in the way of playing articulated passages.

If you watch a garden sprinkler shooting water in a directed stream, it rotates by means on a spring loaded metal plate that, at a particular point in the cycle, slaps into the nozzle, rotating it about 10 degrees. But what causes the plate to move in the first place? A spring is lengthened by the flowing water, which powers the movement to the metal plate. When the valve controlling the water starts to close, the decreasing flow rate causes both the water and the metal plate to slow, then stop.

Comparing this model to a flute, the water is our air, and our tongue is the metal plate. If we put tension into the tongue and mouth, it is like increasing the weight of the metal plate. The heavier plate's increased momentum then makes it harder to change direction. From this, we can conclude that a powerful stream of air, along with a light tongue, is the key to quick playing.

The faster the tonguing, the less the tongue should move. This suggests consonants like "d" and a hard "g" instead of the "t" and "k" commonly taught in the beginning stages of double tonguing. In the most extreme speeds, the tongue almost doesn't move, and the student should not think of the tongue at all.

Singing while playing and how to teach it

Singing while playing is a extended technique that can be used as a diagnostic tool, showing the position of the back of the mouth and throat while playing.

Teaching singing while playing

Because so many flutists do not like to sing, especially younger ones, I suggest an oblique approach to teaching it. Here are the steps I use:

- Say "ooo" as if you are teasing someone.
- Place the hand in front of the mouth and feel the air that comes out with the "oooing". If there is no air, make the sound more breathy.
- Remind the student that air makes the flute go, and, because they can feel air on their hand, the flute will play while they "ooo".
- Place the flute to the lips, and on a low register note, say the "ooo" across the flute. When starting it is always better to have singing with the flute not playing than playing with no singing.
- If the student can sing and play at the same time, have the student start with singing and playing, the release the singing while continuing to blow.
- Finally, play a note with the feeling of singing, but without actually singing.

Diagnostic uses for singing and playing

Singing and playing can be used to show:

- Response in the low register: spot check particularly tricky notes by playing a passage that goes high then low and singing while playing only the low notes.
- Proper transition to the high register: Sing and play a low c. Keeping the singing on the same note while slurring to the next octave c, then continue through the harmonic series with that fingering. If the singing goes away, the throat is closing to cause the jump, which will lead to shrill high register playing.

Use vowel opening, air temperature, and kissing the note and singing will continue throughout the test.
- Loud low register playing: If the throat is closed, the student will not be able to put the volume of air necessary to play loudly. You can't sing with a closed throat, so singing and playing is a great way to train the throat to stay open while forcing more and more air across the flute.

Why we call the key "Thumb Bb", not "Thumb A#", and why it is more of a switch than a key.

Many teachers and directors overcomplicate teaching the thumb Bb key. Compared to many other woodwind instrumentalists, flutists are fortunate to really only have one note that has multiple standard fingerings. However, it is often the source of many arguments amongst flutists and band directors alike. Hopefully, the next couple of paragraphs will help clear up the confusion so we can all move on as a community.

I have, and always will teach, all three fingerings for Bb equally. If a student is uncomfortable with using any of the fingerings for Bb, they will allow their comfort or discomfort with a particular fingering dictate how they approach a sightread passage. All beginning students, when they learn any flat scale, should be able to play that scale using any of the three fingerings equally.

That being said, the thumb Bb is a wonderful addition to the flute. Although it is called a key, it is much more functional to think of it as a switch. On the following diagram, look at the position one and two for the thumb:

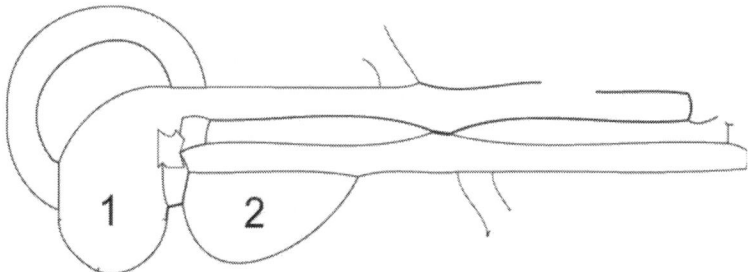

I like to give advice for fingerings as if the student is always sight-reading, as the fingerings will work whether or not there is planning. If you see a Bb in the key signature, have the thumb push in position one any time the thumb is used. For all other cases, use position two. This ensures that any time Bb is approached in flat keys, either from above or below, a Bb sounds and, almost as important, a B natural is avoided. In cases where you do see a B natural in a flat key, it is usually comes from a C, so it is then easy to shift over to position two while the thumb is up for the C.

Notice I did not say that the key was called thumb an A# key. As we know from voice leading, Bb's rarely go to B naturals in a melodic line, but A#'s often resolve to a B natural. For this reason, I do not recommend the thumb Bb for C# and B major when sight reading, as both will have A#'s that resolve to B naturals, or will have accidentals from secondary dominance or the beginning of modulation. There are exceptions to these rules, but they usually require planning ahead of time, so are impractical for sightreading. Also, flutists sometimes slide or rotate their wrist to change temporarily from one thumb position to another. This should be practiced heavily before attempting under pressure and should be thought of as a "last resort", as for those with normal sized hands it creates too many imbalances in posture, leading to other problems.

Vibrato

A disclaimer

Vibrato is one of the most debated topics on the flute, both in how it should sound as well as how it should be taught. I have studied many different ways to produce vibrato, as well as thought deeply about its use, but, after reading this section, you will probably still see a bias. I teach the vibrato I use when playing, as it is my belief that, when done property, it becomes one of the most expressive musical tools on the flute. Also, with the style of vibrato I teach, as long as there is vibrato, the air is always moving with enough energy-- what some people call "fast air".

What is it, and why do we use it?

A preliminary question is "what is sound"? It is amazing how many students do not have at least a working definition of sound. For those of you who need one, or one that makes sense to your students, here you go: sound is jiggling air. Vibrato, then, is a jiggle of the jiggle: either as a frequency modulation, which is a small periodic pitch oscillation, or a small periodic oscillation of the amount and relative strength of the harmonics, otherwise known as oscillating tone color. For purposes of teaching, it is easiest to use this model of frequency modulation, as it is an easy to see this process on stringed instruments-- a finger pivots on the depressed string, oscillating the effective length of the vibrating string.

Where does it come from?

I have answered many questions during clinics, even some crazy ones, including "are you rich?", "is that flute really gold?", and, my favorite: are you always this crazy? However, the physical source of vibrato is one that I never answer, and it is not because I don't know the answer (I do), but because it is harmful for actually learning vibrato. I compare it to looking at your feet while dancing. Also, flutists will pontificate on the sources of vibrato, only to have the vibrato come from a different place when they play. If forced to say something, usually through calling me names, I reply "It depends. However, it is more functional to listen to the result, instead of how it feels. If it sounds right, it is coming from the right place". But, as you can gather, I just don't think it matters, and it can hurt the student's progress, even with the correct information.

Subtractive vs additive vibrato

Using a frequency modulation analysis, we can classify vibrato into two major categories: that which goes flat then in tune, and that which goes sharp. Graphically, they can represented as the following, either going sharp:

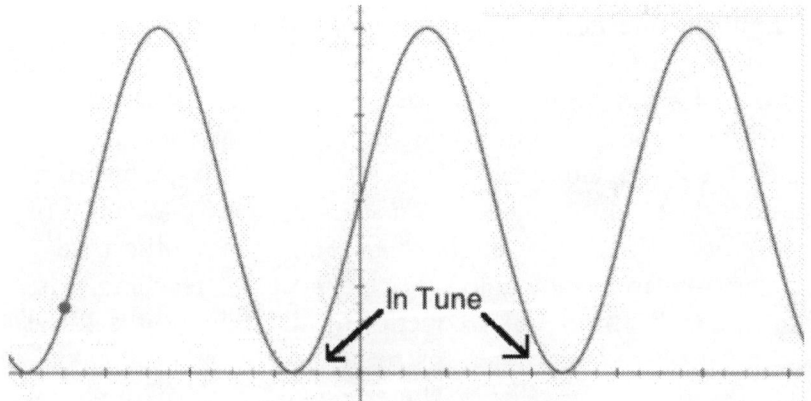

Or subtracting pitch, which goes flat:

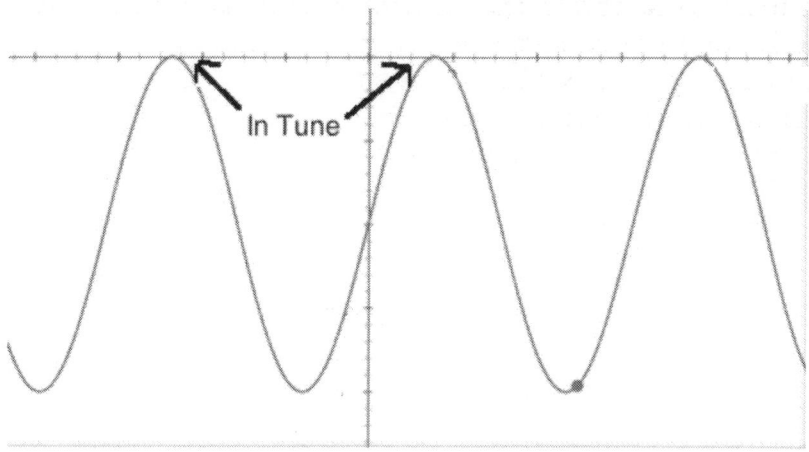

So, one can think of this as either adding something to the sound or removing. I teach the second method.

A metaphor for teaching subtractive vibrato

Imagine you have flat, level ground you wish to make non flat. You can accomplish this one of two ways: you can put piles of dirt on the ground, or you can dig holes. Subtractive vibrato is digging holes in your sound.

Things that can change in vibrato

When we look at vibrato as an oscillating pitch, we can analyze it just like any other periodic wave, so there are two things that can change: the frequency and amplitude. Think of an ocean wave: the frequency is how quickly the ocean waves hit you, and the amplitude is how high the waves are.

Why on the flute?

Compared to other instruments, like the clarinet or oboe, the flute's harmonic spectrum is rather simple. This is one reason the flute sounds pure, as well as why the flute is used in computer music collocation. The simpleness of the spectra allows easy pitch recognition for the computer.

However, this simple harmonic spectra can make the flute sound uninteresting, as you can can't add harmonics to a sound, you can only take them away from the full spectrum available to the instrument. The ear, like the eye, pays more attention to differences, and vibrato, by definition, is a continues series of differentials.

This is the biggest case for using vibrato all of the time. Many times flutists put vibrato as a color on the notes they feel are more important. However, much of the time they end up with the opposite effect: the notes without the vibrato actually stick out more. The flutist, loyal to their model, then uses other means, such as dynamics and rubato, to force the notes with vibrato into the forefront of the phrase. The result is a caricature of how they really want to sound.

Teaching vibrato in 5 minutes or less

I suggest teaching an exaggerated form of additive vibrato, then quickly flipping it to a subtractive form. The steps are as follows:

- Say "who"
- Put your hand up, saying "who" again, feeling the pulse of air. If no air comes out, make the word sound breathy and husky.
- Make the pulse on your hand without saying "who"
- Do a bunch of these in succession, putting a space between each one.
- Connect the pulses with air. You will now have a constant stream of air with piles on top of them. The pulses must have much more air than the connecting air and should be slower than normal speed range for vibrato.

- Put the flute up to the lips, and, on your favorite note, pulse with connected air. If you don't allow the shiny thing to interfere with the last work, it should sound quite comical-- a slow, exaggerated caricature of vibrato. I call this "spaceship vibrato".
- Imagine now that the pulses are the rim of a wheel. When a wheel spins, it does not get smaller. Let the pulses speed up while keeping them big. You will know if the process is being forced if there is not a smooth increase in the speed: if the pulses pause, then start up again very quickly, this is feedback to start over, as the vibrato has changed.
- As the speed increases, start to dig holes into the sound. The pulses now are what is left over from the connecting air.

Using vibrato when the fingers move

Just like with air, students will associate the vibrato with what the fingers are doing. To counteract this, play a single note with a strong vibrato while thinking about moving the fingers. Next, blow with that same air/vibrato, then move the fingers in the pattern required by the music.

In the absence of a really good reason, always use vibrato when you blow

This could really be rule #11. Many people misread this as "you should put vibrato on every note", but this would be a violation of rule #8.

For melodic passages, notes are not discrete objects in time, and have nothing to do with the air, so it is not helpful to take each note separately and sprinkle some vibrato on it. In my model, vibrato is a part of the flute sound, so not hearing vibrato is not the absence of vibrato, but rather a point in time when the vibrato is too slow or small to observe.

Vibrato in the flute section

Just as good string sections in the orchestra use vibrato for a lush sound, so should the flute section of a band. To start, tell the students they use vibrato at any speed they wish, as long as it is not the same speed as the person sitting on either side of them.

Think of vibrato before you play

Continuing our analogy to string playing, have you noticed that good violinists start to pivot their fingers before drawing the bow? The vibrato then starts right when the tone begins. Flutists should embrace a similar thought process. Thinking of the vibrato starting before the note will help move the air correctly for the attack, as well as bring a subtle quality to the interpretation.

Playing in the three registers, as well as transitioning between them

Rules six and seven both deal with playing in the three octaves, but directors often ask me for more advice on playing high and low on the instrument, especially when working with beginners.

Think temperature of air for octave, amount of air for dynamics

I describe the quality of air in the low register to be hot, and that of the middle and high registers as cold. I prefer not to talk of air speed because the opposite of fast is slow, and, to most students, slow air connotes less air for the low notes. It is very effective to tell a student to make the air colder on their hand, then use that same air to play an octave higher.

Putting more air into the flute puts more energy into the instrument. We hear this as louder playing. So more air equals loud, less air equals soft. We now have four combinations available to us, shown in the following matrix:

	Cold	*Hot*
More Air	Loud and High	Loud and Low
Less Air	Soft and High	Soft and Low

Matrix of air amount and temperature

Using these guidelines as a base, we can make things easier and faster by applying kiss the note, vowel opening, and playing out the nose, as the effects are additive: the air will not have to be as cold for the note to break into the higher octave, or so hot to have low notes come out. This flexibility, caused by stacking different methods towards the same goal, not only increases confidence in the player, but also gives options for tone colors at any given dynamic and register.

Quick changes from high to low

Students often have trouble quickly moving from the 3rd to 1st octaves rapidly, limiting the speed of some technical passages. The solution lies in the ability to change register using more than one process simultaneously. Here is the process I teach:

- Determine in the passage which notes speak less easily.

- Think of the setup in the body which causes those harder notes to speak. This includes vowel opening, amount of kiss to the note, and where the tone should resonate in the body.

- Play the entire passage with the body setup for the harder notes to speak, and allow the easier ones to speak just by thinking they will come out. The body will make micro adjustments to cause the change.

Students can also train this in their technical studies, such as arpeggios and etudes. The register shifts becomes dynamic, automatically setting the body up for the more difficult sets of notes in a passage, then applying unconscious micro changes to the particular note played. At the highest level, high and low blur. There is just air, sculpted into music.

Words I never use, with explanation

Words are only meaningful if both parties using the word can agree on the meaning. The following is a list of words don't always mean how they are used, so I find they have limited use in teaching.

Talent

This is the easiest, so starting with it makes sense. If you call a person "talented", they stop working. If you call a person "untalented", they stop working. So, if your goal is to have your students not work, use the word talent when you teach.

Try

This one is fun, because it causes the most arguments from others, and I learned it from a little green alien who lived in a swamp. I have no use for unnecessary words, as they only serve to dilute meaning and confuse the student.

If a word has function, especially if it is an action, you can show me what the word is by doing it, right? So, try to pick up a book. There are only two options, you will either succeed in picking up the book, or you will fail to pick the book. The scary thing is that you can add the word "try" into both the case where you fail and where you fail.

We usually use the word in situations where we think there a risk of failure. So, trying presupposes failure.

I prefer to live in a world where people do things. When they succeed, they celebrate. When they fail, they use their mind to figure out what went wrong, so they can be confident it doesn't happen again. Trying has no place in that world.

Support

Support is another word for which I just don't have a use. Now, before you start yelling at the book, read the rest of the section.

If I were to ask 50 flutists the question "what is support", then I would get 55 different answers. Some flutists would ask someone to firm one part of the abs, others would ask to push the abs out, others would ask to suck the abs in. Other should talk about the intercostal muscles... you get the drift.

If you are a flute teacher reading this book, you might be thinking "well, I understand it better, and this is how you do it...", that is great, but remember that there will be someone else who believes the same thing about the opposite physical process and is probably as correct as you are. Often, the definition of all of the anatomy we describe when teaching is either too ambiguous to be useful or so cumbersome it gets into the way of teaching.

Also, when told to a students who do not do the "support thing" all by themselves, they just tense up. So the student either already does the thing we want them to or they don't, and we use a word that causes more tension, the enemy of quality flute playing. What again is the point of this word?

A better metaphor: back to the balloon

If I blow up a balloon, the balloon pushes back on the air inside. The more air I put into the balloon, the more the balloon will push air out with great force to start, then taper off as the elastic returns to normal.

People are like balloons. When you breathe in beyond your normal tidal volume, all of the associated fascia stretches as well, wanting to bring the body back to its non stretched state. So, instead of teaching support, teach your students to drink deeply and often from the air around them, then release that air without pause across the flute.

Conclusion, and a challenge

At at its base, this book is more than a collection of tips. I have always liked to solve problems, which is one of the wonderful things about teaching. If you approach teaching the right way, it is the most challenging of problems: communicating to the net generation what we know. The good news is, as the most important work anyone can do, it is worth more than every once we can give.

The heart of this book, however, goes beyond this. Teaching is an evolving process, and should always be treated with joy. The paradigms in this book work, so I chose to share them with you. I challenge you use them in the creative way they were intended, and, in the application, find more effective and efficient models then I have presented here. Then, I hope you share them with others.

If you have any comments or questions about what you have read in the book, feel free to contact me: I am passionate about teaching and love to talk and debate ways of communicating knowledge. I can be reached via email at gotflute@me.com.

About the Author

A student of Jeffery Khaner and Jean Larson, Mr. Jason Blank has a Bachelor of Music from Southern Methodist University. He has performed concertos with the Delaware Symphony, the Texas A&M Orchestra, the Wilmington Orchestra, and was a finalist to perform with the Philadelphia Orchestra as a soloist. He was one of only two freshmen in Southern Methodist's history to win the school concerto competition as a freshman. He has performed in masterclasses for Julius Baker, Brad Gardner, Jeanne Baxtresser, Gary Schocker, and Marzio Conti. He has also performed with Voices of Change, the Irving Symphony Orchestra, the Brazos Valley Symphony, and played in the orchestra for the Graz, Austria vocal festival. Jason has been a Guest Artist/lecturer at the National Flute Association Annual Convention, as well as flute festivals and educator conferences in Florida, Oklahoma, Texas, and New England.

While in Texas, Mr. Blank had a successful teaching studio in first the Dallas then Houston markets, teaching up at 100 students a week. Jason served as both a product manager and artist for the Wm S. Haynes flute company, performing for and educating students first in Texas, then throughout North America. A specialist in working with high school and middle school students, Jason has developed a system for non-flutist band directors to see instant and lasting changes in their flute section.

After leaving Haynes, Mr. Blank became the sole distributer for Bernhard Hammig handmade instruments throughout North America, as well a marketing and sales consultant to other music related business. He also is a partner in the Fluterscooter case cover line, as well as the Green Golly Project, a protean initiative for saving music education in America.

Jason can be contacted through his email: gotflute@me.com

Made in the USA
Charleston, SC
02 August 2012